MARY OLIVER,
HOLDING ON TO WONDER

Erin Frankel

illustrated by
Jasu Hu

CALKINS CREEK
AN IMPRINT OF ASTRA BOOKS FOR YOUNG READERS
New York

Mary Oliver was in a beautiful place.
It was not far from home, but to Mary, it felt like another world, a softer world that came to life in Mary's hands with a notebook and pen.

But it all began with *wonder*.

In the forest, she wondered about the birds
and the lilies
and the water in the stream
and about all the things that could not speak
yet somehow spoke to Mary.
Maybe they too felt sad sometimes. Or lonely.

Mary had many questions.
  How would it feel to be a forest creature—
  or to have wings and fly?
  Is the center of a flower called the heart?
  Are rocks somehow alive?

But what Mary really wanted to know was how to take this place with her—wherever she might go. This place where she felt free. This place that sang to her like the poems in her books.

Maybe *poetry* was the key.

Mary noticed how words pieced together filled her with light. And how some poems felt like they were written just for her. How could this be?

Who were these writers who felt like friends? Had they also loved the woods and listened tenderly?

Mary wondered especially about the amazing, late poet Edna St. Vincent Millay and longed to know the place where her poems found their way.

She wondered so much she wrote a letter
to Edna's sister Norma. She asked if she could visit the
house where Edna had once lived and wrote.

When Norma's letter arrived, one word
sang out joyfully.

It was a word that would open new doors
for Mary once she finished high school.
YES!

After several visits, Norma invited Mary to stay. Edna had left many papers behind, and there was much to organize. Would Mary like the job?

For a young poet like Mary, the answer was sure to be . . .

YES!

But to Mary, what lived beyond walls was always more exciting. In nature, her imagination could run free. In the quiet, questions would unfold.

And in each moment, Mary found something to notice and listen to.

Each moment was a mystery.

Mary's notes took her back to the tiniest instant—an idea, a feeling—that she could grow into a poem. She searched for verses and lines and words that felt right. It took hours and hours to bring a poem to light!

Mary began to wonder if her poems
might speak to others just as many poems
had spoken to her. Poetry had always been a gift to Mary,
so she decided to share *her* gift with the world.

When Mary met photographer
Molly Malone Cook, she was
amazed by Molly's gift to the world.
Were they asking the same
questions about life?

Like how the sun must feel when it folds itself slowly, gently back into the sky or how it feels to be wild and free and how pictures and words might capture such beautiful things . . .

Someone once told Mary she used the word *beautiful*
too much in her poems. But Mary wrote what she could see.
And in her new life with Molly on the shores of Cape Cod,
Mary saw beauty.

Mary thought dogs were *extra* beautiful. She noticed how they lived each moment *joyfully*.

Notebook in hand, Mary set out each morning in search of wonder. She hid pencils behind trees so she would always be prepared.

Foxes and moon snails; black bears and owls; snow crickets and goldfinches; sunflowers and ponds— Mary wrote on and on.

Mary's poems spoke to many,
and people started to know her by name.
But Mary wanted her quiet world to
stay the same.
When she won a famous poetry prize, she simply
went about her day. She had work to do. Work that she loved.

That's Mary Oliver!

Other writers were excited to learn from Mary.
So now and then, Mary went away to teach.
But no matter where Mary went, she woke up
early to meet the day with wonder.

She brought her favorite poems. And, of course,
she brought her dog.

To write well, Mary insisted, took lots of noticing.
Rhythm, sound, rhyme, line, repetition, imagery—
there were so many elements of poetry!
There were so many poems yet to read!

Mary's students thought she knew everything. But Mary thought, how boring that would be!

Mary did know that the stones and the sea,
the flowers, the weeds,
the moon, the stars,
the geese, the gulls
welcome us
just as we are.

Mary wondered about life being hard sometimes—especially after Molly died. But as always, poetry made the hard parts softer. And for that, Mary was grateful.

As Mary grew older, she decided to move. It was time for a change. She missed Cape Cod, but the world was still at her fingertips. So Mary did what she knew best.

She noticed

and listened

and wondered,

then wrote poems that longed to be told—

poems meant for *everyone*.

Because Mary Oliver hoped that there was someone
just like you
on the other side of her words
holding on to wonder
just like Mary.

AUTHOR'S NOTE

The exceptional beauty of Mary Oliver's writings inspired me to learn more about her life.

Listening to Mary's interviews, studying her writing, and walking where she once walked in Provincetown, Cape Cod, helped transport me into her world in my imagination. I couldn't help but feel that Mary was a kindred spirit. Like her, my childhood was steeped in nature. Like Mary, I tucked away into quiet places and poems whenever I could.

Knowing that Mary was a deeply private person, I approached her story with respect and intention, focusing on the parts of Mary's life that she came back to time and again through writing and telling. Following Mary's wisdom, I paid attention.

Mary Oliver (1935–2019) is one of our country's most beloved poets. Her poems earned her the Pulitzer Prize and the National Book Award among many other honors. They teach us how to walk slowly through the world noticing; they fill us with wonder; they linger and belong, as Mary believed, to everyone.

For Mary, nature and poetry offered an escape from the sadness of her childhood in Ohio where she was born and grew up. She spoke of how poetry saved her by allowing her to reimagine a world of beauty. After high school, Mary seized an opportunity to immerse herself in words at Steepletop, home of the late poet Edna St. Vincent Millay, in Austerlitz, New York.

As a rising poet, Mary spent several years in England and New York City, eventually moving to Provincetown, Cape Cod, where she lived and wrote for five decades. She found beauty, mystery, and inspiration for poems in the New England landscape and led a simple life in which she had the freedom and time to wonder and write. Mary went away to teach from time to time. How lucky for the students in her classroom, and yet her poems—so often

instructions for life—allow us all to be her students.

While it was no secret that Mary preferred the company of animals and nature to people, her relationship with photographer Molly Malone Cook brought her closer to the joy and kindness of the human world. Together they shared a curiosity for the mysteries of life. All this against the backdrop of their beloved world in Cape Cod.

Mary did not have all the answers to her questioning, nor did she want them. To wonder and rejoice in the unknown was much more interesting. We all start out as children wondering, but it isn't easy to hold on to wonder in a world that favors knowing over not knowing. Holding on to wonder was the life work of Mary Oliver. Her words remind us that it can be our work too.

I felt the call to write this book because I see beauty not only *in* Mary Oliver's poems, but *because* of her poems. I wish I had discovered Mary Oliver as a child. What more might I have felt or seen had her poetry accompanied me? I hope that in these pages and beyond, you too will wonder about the beauty that Mary Oliver chose to see and share with the world.

TIMELINE

1935 Mary Jane Oliver is born on September 10 in Cleveland, Ohio.

1945 Inspired by nature and books by favorite poets, Mary begins to experiment with writing poetry.

1953 Mary writes a letter to Norma Millay, sister of the late poet Edna St. Vincent Millay, asking permission to visit Edna's home, Steepletop, in Austerlitz, New York. Edna was the first female poet to be awarded the Pulitzer Prize for Poetry, in 1923.

1953 The day after high school graduation, Mary visits Steepletop for the first time. After several more visits, Mary accepts an invitation to stay and help organize Edna's papers. The setting inspires many new poems.

1958 Moves to New York City. On a return visit to Steepletop, Mary meets photographer Molly Malone Cook, who will one day become her lifelong partner.

1963 Lives in England for a short time and publishes her first book of poetry, *No Voyage and Other Poems*. Mary will publish a new book every one or two years thereafter.

1964 Mary joins Molly in Provincetown, Massachusetts, which will become home for the next five decades. Mary's poetry finds its roots in the Cape Cod landscape.

1972 Receives a National Endowment of the Arts fellowship.

1980 Becomes a Guggenheim fellow in poetry.

1983 Teaches at Case Western Reserve University. Mary will also teach at Bucknell University, University of Cincinnati, Sweet Briar College, and Bennington College, where she will hold the Catherine Osgood Foster Chair for Distinguished Teaching.

1984 Receives the Pulitzer Prize for Poetry for her book *American Primitive*.

1992 Receives the National Book Award for her publication *New and Selected Poems, Volume One*.

1998 Receives the Lannan Literary Award for Lifetime Achievement.

1998 Receives honorary doctorate from the Art Institute of Boston. Mary will go on to receive honorary doctorates from Dartmouth College, Tufts University, and Marquette University.

2005 Molly dies. Two years later, Mary shares the story of their love and life together in *Our World*.

2012 Mary is diagnosed with lung cancer, which she will write about in her poem "The Fourth Sign of the Zodiac."

2014 Moves to Florida after deciding that it is time for a change.

2015 Publishes her last book of poetry, *Felicity*.

2019 Mary dies on January 17 in Hobe Sound, Florida. The gift of her words lives on.

A NOTE ON THE CRAFT OF POETRY

When it comes to sound, how can tools like alliteration, assonance, or onomatopoeia change the feel of a poem? How do metaphor and simile build a picture in the reader's mind? What gives a poem rhythm? What are the different types of rhyme?

As a lifetime student of poetry, Mary Oliver thought deeply about such questions. And as a distinguished poetry teacher, she encouraged students to do the same. In Mary's books *A Poetry Handbook* and *Rules for the Dance,* she walks readers through poetic devices including those mentioned in this book—rhythm, sound, rhyme, line, repetition, imagery—and points to examples from her favorite poems. For younger poets looking to explore the craft of poetry writing, the Poetry Foundation (poetryfoundation.org/learn/children) has beginner resources for children and teens including poems, learning activities, poetry readings, and a glossary of poetic terms.

SELECT BIBLIOGRAPHY

Barks, Coleman, host. "Mary Oliver, Reading, 4 August 2001." Lannan Foundation, August 4, 2001. lannan.org/media/mary-oliver-with-coleman-barks.

Beacon Broadside. "Mary Oliver on Edna St. Vincent Millay." October 19, 2007, beaconbroadside.com/broadside/2007/10/edna-st-vincent.html.

Franklin, Ruth. "What Mary Oliver's Critics Don't Understand." *New Yorker*, November 20, 2017.

Poetry Foundation. "Mary Oliver." poetryfoundation.org/poets/mary-oliver.

Ratiner, Steven. "Poet Mary Oliver: A Solitary Walk." *Christian Science Monitor*, December 9, 1992, csmonitor.com/1992/1209/09161.html.

Shriver, Maria. "Maria Shriver Interviews the Famously Private Mary Oliver." *Oprah*, March 9, 2011, oprah.com/entertainment/maria-shriver-interviews-poet-mary-oliver/all#ixzz7BAXw4OnA.

Tippett, Krista, host. "Mary Oliver Listening to the World." On Being, February 5, 2015, onbeing.org/programs/mary-oliver-listening-to-the-world/. Transcript.

"Watch: A Tribute to Mary Oliver." WBUR, May 2, 2019, wbur.org/events/461193/ a-tribute-to-mary-oliver.

ACKNOWLEDGMENTS

To the writers whose work has informed my research, I thank you. To the creative spirits, includung Susan Cohen, Carolyn Yoder, and my editor, Rebecca Davis, who saw something special in the original draft and encouraged me to keep going—thank you for holding on to wonder. Appreciation to Marc Harshman, children's book author and Poet Laureate of West Virginia, for sharing his insight on this project. I reserve my deepest gratitude for Mary Oliver. I found inspiration and insight in Mary's writing, including all her books as well as the select poems, prose, and notes listed below. It would be impossible to include everything, yet everything deserves a place. I hope you will explore Mary's writing and that her words will speak to you as deeply as they do to me.

"A Pretty Song" [*Thirst: Poems*. Boston: Beacon Press, 2006.]

"Bone" [*Why I Wake Early: New Poems*. Boston: Beacon Press, 2004.]

"Do Stones Feel" [*Blue Horses: Poems*. New York: Penguin Press, 2014.]

"How Everything Adores Being Alive" [*Why I Wake Early: New Poems*. Boston: Beacon Press, 2004.]

"I Happened To Be Standing" [*A Thousand Mornings*. New York: Penguin Books, 2013.]

"Just as the Calendar Began to Say Summer" [*Devotions: The Selected Poems of Mary Oliver*. New York: Penguin Press, 2017.]

"Lead" [*New and Selected Poems: Volume Two*. Boston: Beacon Press, 1992.]

"Mary Oliver on Edna St. Vincent Millay" [Beacon Broadside, October 19, 2007. beaconbroadside.com/broadside/2007/10/edna-st-vincent.html.]

"Pen and Paper and a Breath of Fresh Air" [*Blue Pastures*. New York: Harcourt Brace, 1995.]

"Praying" [*Thirst: Poems*. Boston: Beacon Press, 2006.]

"Sleeping in the Forest" [*Twelve Moons*. Boston: Little, Brown, 1979.]

"Snow Geese" [*Why I Wake Early: New Poems*. Boston: Beacon Press, 2004.]

"Some Questions You Might Ask" [*House of Light*. Boston: Beacon Press, 1990.]

"Some Things Say the Wise One" [*Why I Wake Early: New Poems*. Boston: Beacon Press, 2004.]

"Sometimes" [*Red Bird: Poems*. Boston: Beacon Press, 2008.]

"Spring" [*House of Light*. Boston: Beacon Press, 1990.]

"Staying Alive." [Essay. In *Blue Pastures*. San Diego: Harcourt Brace, 1995.]

"Steepletop." [Essay. In *Blue Pastures*. San Diego: Harcourt Brace, 1995.]

"The Messenger" [*Thirst: Poems*. Boston: Beacon Press, 2006.]

"The Moth, The Mountains, The Rivers" [*A Thousand Mornings*. New York: Penguin Books, 2013.]

"The Singular and Cheerful Life" [*Evidence: Poems*. Boston: Beacon Press, 2009.]

"The Summer Day" [*House of Light*. Boston: Beacon Press, 1990.]

"The Sun" [*New and Selected Poems*. Boston: Beacon Press, 1992.]

"Today" [*A Thousand Mornings*. New York: Penguin Books, 2013.]

"When I am Among the Trees" [*Devotions: The Selected Poems of Mary Oliver*. New York: Penguin Press, 2017.]

"Why I Wake Early" [*Why I Wake Early: New Poems*. Boston: Beacon Press, 2004.]

"Wild Geese" [*Dream Work*. Boston: Atlantic Monthly Press, 1986.]

To my daughters, Gabriela, Sofia, and Kelsey—
you will always be my most beautiful poem.
And to Alvaro—for believing in me. —*EF*

To Rebecca and Erin, who invited me to join
this incredible journey. To the sky and the earth,
which lead everything together. —*JH*

For information about permission to reproduce selections from this book,
please contact permissions@astrapublishinghouse.com.

Calkins Creek
An imprint of Astra Books for Young Readers,
a division of Astra Publishing House
astrapublishinghouse.com
Printed in China

ISBN: 978-1-6626-8082-3 (hc)
ISBN: 978-1-6626-8081-6 (eBook)
Library of Congress Control Number: 2024947158

First edition

10 9 8 7 6 5 4 3 2 1

Design by Barbara Grzeslo
The text is set in Avenir LT Std.
The art is created digitally emulating watercolor technique.